The Great Schism: The History and Legacy of the Split Between the Catholic and Eastern Orthodox Churches in 1054

By Charles River Editors

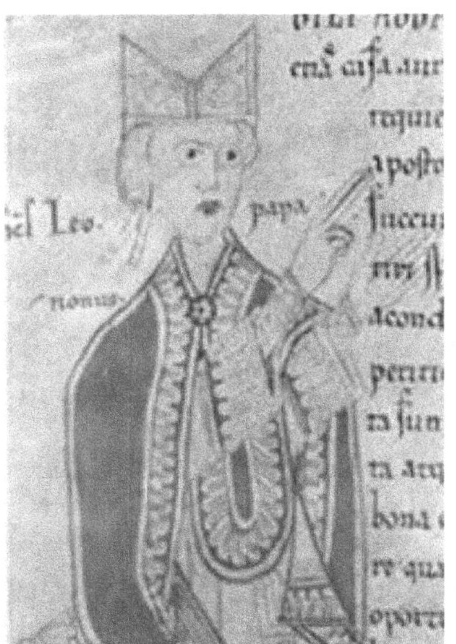

Pope Leo IX

About Charles River Editors

Charles River Editors is a boutique digital publishing company, specializing in bringing history back to life with educational and engaging books on a wide range of topics. Keep up to date with our new and free offerings with this 5 second sign up on our weekly mailing list, and visit Our Kindle Author Page to see other recently published Kindle titles.

We make these books for you and always want to know our readers' opinions, so we encourage you to leave reviews and look forward to publishing new and exciting titles each week.

Introduction

A mosaic of Jesus in the Hagia Sophia

"My dearest brother, we do not deny to the Roman Church the primacy amongst the five sister Patriarchates; and we recognize her right to the most honorable seat at an Ecumenical Council. But she has separated herself from us by her own deeds, when through pride she assumed a monarchy which does not belong to her office... How shall we accept decrees from her that have been issued without consulting us and even without our knowledge? If the Roman Pontiff, seated on the lofty throne of his glory, wishes to thunder at us and, so to speak, hurl his mandates at us from on high, and if he wishes to judge us and even to rule us and our Churches, not by taking counsel with us but at his own arbitrary pleasure, what kind of brotherhood, or even what kind of parenthood can this be? We should be the slaves, not the sons, of such a Church, and the Roman See would not be the pious mother of sons but a hard and imperious mistress of slaves." Nicetas, Archbishop of Nicomedia in the 12th century

For nearly a thousand years following its foundation, there was only one Christian Church. Centered in the city of Rome, the Church expanded and grew until it became the dominant religion in Europe and beyond. The early growth of the Church had been suppressed by the Romans until the Emperor Constantine became the first to convert the empire to Christianity, and from that point forward, the growth of the Church Was inextricably linked with the Roman Empire, the most powerful military, economic, and political force in the ancient world.

For almost 600 years, from the defeat of Carthage in the Second Punic War in 201 BCE to around 395 CE, Rome was one of the most important cities in the world, but things were beginning to change around the time Constantine converted the empire. Rome controlled large areas of the world, but by the 4th century the emphasis had shifted from military conquest to the control of lucrative trade routes. The problem was that the city of Rome, isolated in the southern half of the Italian peninsula, was far from these routes, and this compelled Constantine to establish a major Roman city on the site of ancient Byzantium. The new city, Constantinople, was located on a strategic site controlling the narrow straits between the Black Sea and the Aegean, meaning it was firmly astride some of the most important trade routes in the ancient world between Europe and Asia and between the Mediterranean and the Black Sea.

Constantinople became the second most important city of the Roman Empire, thriving in parallel with Rome, but then the empire split into Eastern and Western provinces, with Constantinople the capital of the east and Rome the capital of the west. Control of trade routes made Constantinople increase in power and influence while Rome became less important.

In 476, the process was completed when Rome was attacked and sacked by invading Goths, while Constantinople survived the foreign invasions, mainly by paying large bribes to keep the Goths and Huns at bay. Power shifted entirely to Constantinople, and the Latin-speaking Roman Empire evolved into the Greek-speaking Byzantine Empire. Rome, once the most important city in the world, was all but abandoned.

However, not all power and influence shifted east, because one important institution remained firmly linked with the city of Rome: the Bishops of the Church. Under the rule of previous emperors, Christian Bishops had not only been formally recognized, but had been given power within the Roman state. The most important of all was "*I Sommi Pontefici Romani*" the supreme pontiff of Rome. The earliest holders of this title were martyrs and saints of the Church, but by the time of the rise of Constantinople, this role was elected by the other Bishops of the Church. This role would later become known as the Pope (from the Greek word "*pappas*" meaning "father"), but even before that title was adopted, the Supreme Pontiff in Rome was widely recognized as the leader of the Church. In historical terms, these early leaders of the Church are often referred to as "popes" even though that title was not formally adopted until after the division the Church.

Rome's preeminence was not a situation that was welcomed in Constantinople, now the center of the Byzantine Empire and a thriving and wealthy metropolis. After being sacked by outsiders, Rome had become a virtual ghost town, partially ruined and inhabited by a small number of hardy survivors, yet in center of the crumbling city was the Vatican Borgo, the Palace of the Supreme Pontiff and the heart of the Church. In retrospect, it is easy to see that this was a situation that was bound to lead to conflict and disagreement, with the Greek-speaking Eastern Orthodox Church centered in Constantinople and being governed by Latin-speaking popes in a faraway city. Moreover, there had already been theological disputes as far back as Constantine's time, which had led to the famous Council of Nicaea in the 4th century CE.

This situation would lead to growing theological and temporal differences between the two branches of the Church until this finally exploded into a complete breakdown of relations and the splitting of the once unified Christian Church into two different and separate churches. This is the story of that split, the Great Schism of 1054.

The Great Schism: The History and Legacy of the Split Between the Catholic and Eastern Orthodox Churches in 1054 chronicles the events that led to the schism, the key figures that played a hand in the confusion, and how the contentious issues were finally resolved. Along with pictures depicting important people, places, and events, you will learn about the Great Schism like never before.

The Expansion of the Church across the Roman Empire

The growth of Christianity is irrevocably linked with the legacy of the Roman Empire, in particular the reign of Emperor Constantine the Great. Not much is known about the early years of Constantine's life, or his upbringing. As the son of a family who at least on his father's side possessed a significant degree of wealth and social standing, he was presumably educated in the traditional fashion of the Roman aristocracy, with tutors lecturing him in history, philosophy and the sciences. He was likely also taught music, riding, and the arts of war: combat, strategy and tactics.

An ancient bust of Constantine now housed at the Metropolitan Museum of Art in New York City

In 284 CE, when Constantine would have been around 12 years old, the Emperor Diocletian made Constantius governor of Dalmatia, a signal honor which meant a vast increase in the family's wealth and influence. The following year, Diocletian made the momentous decision to appoint the prominent general Maximian as his co-emperor, effectively starting the great schism which would eventually see the two halves of the empire become two completely separate entities. Diocletian took the East and established himself in Nicomedia (modern Turkey) as his new capital, while Maximian ruled the West from Mediolanum (Milan). Although the separation was made for purely practical administrative reasons and the Empire was continuously described as indivisible, the seeds of separation had been sown. Constantius, however, was one of the men who benefitted most from Diocletian's decision due to being an intimate associate of Maximian. Three years after the split, he was raised to the newly created post of praetorian prefect, a sort of subordinate emperor who could act with Maximian's authority.

Bust of Diocletian

Bust of Maximian

Constantius prospered under the new regime by assuming control of the rich province of Gaul, and to strengthen his ties with Maximian he cast Helena aside and married Maximian's stepdaughter Theodora. Constantine, who was deeply attached to his mother, was in all likelihood furious, but there was nothing he could do; the political advantages of a marriage to Theodora were undeniable. In 293 CE, Constantius packed both Helena and Constantine and sent them off to Diocletian's court in Nicomedia, possibly so he could enjoy his newly wedded bliss but also for another, more pragmatic reason. Diocletian had divided the empire still further, splitting the two parts into two further units and granting two Caesars, newly created "sub-emperors," absolute power over the two units respectively, though they would still be subordinated to Diocletian and Maximian. These two Caesars were Constantius and Galerius, a man who had an unsavory reputation for being a brute. Thus, Constantine would be a hostage for his father's good behavior at Diocletian's court.

Bust of Galerius

In the wake of a prophecy from the vastly influential oracle at Delphi, Diocletian began what became known as the "Great Persecution" of the Christians. The Christians, whose worship excluded the divinity of other gods (unlike the polytheist pagans, who might consider other gods inferior but never denied their very existence), made a convenient scapegoat, and their church in Nicomedia was torn down. At the same time, known Christians were deprived of their public offices, and Christian clerics were arrested. Constantine later professed deep disgust at Diocletian's actions and attempted to distance himself from them, but he seems to have been ambivalent to them at the time. He was a prominent figure at court, and although he was in many ways a hostage and thus could not challenge Diocletian, he was obviously in the Emperor's good graces at the time since he secured a promotion to *tribunus ordini primi* (tribune of the first order) in 305.

The same year Constantine obtained his promotion, Diocletian fell ill, and he decided to step down as Emperor rather than be driven to his deathbed by the cares of the state. However, rather than favor Constantine and Maximian's son Maxentius in the succession, as everybody expected, Diocletian was manipulated by Galerius into choosing Constantius and himself as the two new Emperors. An able but uninspiring general named Severus was chosen as Caesar of the West, while Maximinus, the son of Galerius's half-sister, was chosen as Galerius's Caesar. Constantine and Maxentius were snubbed.

Maxentius

Constantine soon realized that staying at court was not only likely to get him passed over for further promotion but might also cost him his life. Galerius heaped ever more dangerous and demanding tasks upon him, including combat with wild beasts and detached reconnaissance behind enemy lines, clearly aimed at getting him killed and disposing of a rival. In the end, Constantine decided he would be safest with his father, so he requested permission to join him. He connived to get Galerius obscenely drunk while he considered the proposal, and once he secured his acquiescence he fled the city with only a small escort, half-killing a string of horses in the process, to put as much distance between himself and Galerius before the latter sobered up sufficiently to regret his decision. He joined his father at his armed camp in Bononia (Boulogne) shortly afterwards.

From Bononia, Constantius and Constantine sailed to Britannia and marched northwards to Eboracum (York), which held the largest garrison in Northern Britain. At the head of the Eboracum troops, Constantius and Constantine campaigned jointly north of Hadrian's Wall against the Picts but met with little success as the Picts fell back northwards, using unconventional guerrilla warfare tactics and refusing to be drawn into pitched battle. Eventually the army marched back to Eboracum without having achieved much, other than to worsen an illness that had afflicted Constantius for years. He died at Eboracum in the summer of 306, after having asserted his support for Constantine's claim to take the title of Augustus in his stead and become Galerius's co-Emperor. Chrocus, King of the Alamanni and commander of Constantius's auxiliaries, confirmed Constantius's appointment, as did the legions that had owed fealty to Constantius. Constantine sent a message proclaiming his new status to Galerius, who fell into a rage and denied any such appointment, instead proclaiming Severus as Augustus and declaring that Constantine would have to make do with the rank of Caesar. In order to avoid civil war, Constantine had to grudgingly accept.

 Despite the support of the legions of Gaul, Britain and Iberia, Constantine knew his new position was far from secure, so he quickly set about repairing the infrastructure of his new domains, expanding military bases and supply depots and resurfacing the crucial roads between them to guarantee rapid troop movement. He then returned to Augusta Treverorum, the western Caesar's capital (in modern Trier, France), just in time to repel an invasion of the Franks under their kings Meirogasus and Ascaric.

The Franks had hoped to profit from Constantius's death by taking the untried Constantine unawares, but they found him more than ready. Not only did he drive their forces back over the Rhine, he also captured Meirogasus and Ascaric and fed them to wild beasts in Augusta Treverorum's amphitheater, along with other prisoners of war (which it should be noted does not suggest a particularly Christian sensibility). However, Constantine, though not especially adept at aping Christian morals, was far more skilled at currying favor with them. While Galerius was engaged in a series of ruthless persecutions against the Christians in his portion of the Roman Empire, Constantine, in order to prove how much more enlightened he was than his rival, extended a policy of tolerance and reconciliation towards all Christians within his portion of the Western Roman Empire. He accomplished this by reinstating lands and titles that had been lost during the great persecution, as well as preaching religious tolerance. He also undertook a major renovation and expansion of Augusta Treverorum, increasing its fortifications and beginning work on a palatial complex within the walls. Other cities throughout Gaul also benefited from his renovations projects, which boosted the economy within his borders.

If things were improving within Constantine's domains, however, trouble was stirring beyond his borders. Maxentius, who had taken up residence in Rome and was building a powerful army of his supporters there, received the news of Constantine's appointment as Caesar by declaring him the illegitimate offspring of a foreign whore and refusing to acknowledge his title's legitimacy, thereby proclaiming himself Emperor.

Maxentius was not the only one who believed he would win a civil war, for it was widely believed within Constantine's own inner circle that an attack on Maxentius would fail. The omens, which were notoriously fickle (unless manipulated by a skilled politician), suggested a gloomy outlook, but Constantine ignored all such dire warnings and remained determined to attack.

In the first months of 312, when campaigning season resumed, Constantine took an expeditionary force of 40,000 men through the high passes and into the Alps. He then marched on Segusium (Susa, Italy), the first of a series of vital fortresses manned by Maxentian troops along his line of march. Despite formidable defenses and the refusal of the garrison to come to terms, Constantine's troops made short work of the fortress, burning the gates down and storming the walls. Constantine, however, kept his men rigidly in check and spared the inhabitants of Segusium the horrors that traditionally followed a siege, a calculated move that helped his reputation skyrocket throughout northern Italy.

Eventually, Maxentius realized he had no choice but to offer battle, and after constructing a bridge of boats across the Tiber, in October of 312 Maxentius marched his army over the river to face Constantine in open battle. Despite the attrition of the year's campaigns and widespread desertion, Maxentius could still field double the number of troops that Constantine possessed, but if myth and Constantine's later propaganda can be believed, Constantine possessed an invincible ally: God.

According to both Eusebius and Lactantius, two of the Emperor's principal biographers, the day before the battle Constantine was stricken by a vision. Lactantius claims that Constantine was visited by an angel as he dreamt the night before battle, while Eusebius's version is even more theatrical. According to Eusebius, while Constantine's army was on the march, a fiery symbol, shaped like the crossed X and P of the Latin Alphabet (☧) and bearing beneath it the legend "*Εν Τούτῳ Νίκα*" ("by this sign, you will conquer"), appeared in the sky above. The X and P represented the Greek letters Xhi and Rho, the first two letters of Christ's name in the Greek spelling.

Presumably, such a divine manifestation would have prompted an on-the-spot conversion, and Constantine certainly alluded to that in later propaganda, but there is significant evidence that the original manifestation was actually viewed as a pagan divine revelation. In that version, the revelation was interpreted as being the halo of *Sol Invictus,* the Sun God with whom Constantine claimed a long-standing association and whose iconography was depicted in coins issued by Constantine even years after the battle.

This gold coin, minted in 313, depicts Constantine with *Sol Invictus*

One problem with the theory that Constantine merely observed what he thought was a divine revelation from *Sol Invictus* is that accounts agree he changed the appearance of his equipment before the battle. Some scholars have rather optimistically suggested that the fiery symbol was in fact a sun dog, but whatever the source of Constantine's divine inspiration, whether miraculous, scientific or simply clever propaganda, on the day of battle his armies apparently approached Maxentius's forces with the Xhi Rho painted on their shields. According to Eusebius: "Assuming therefore the Supreme God as his patron, and invoking His Christ to be his preserver and aid, and setting the victorious trophy, the salutary symbol, in front of his soldiers and body-guard, he marched with his whole forces, trying to obtain again for the Romans the freedom they had inherited from their ancestors."

After he won the decisive battle, Constantine entered Rome the following day in a formal victory parade which was apparently met by throngs of people in genuine jubilation. Maxentius's body had been found and pulled out of the river the day before, and his head was paraded at the front of Constantine's victory column. Interestingly, Constantine declined to make the traditional victory offerings at the Temple of Jupiter, but this may not necessarily be proof of his Christian conversion so much as it might either reflect his continuing attachment to *Sol Invictus* or his awareness that such a gesture would alienate Rome's Christians. Constantine then subjected Maxentius to a *damnatio memoriae*, as he had done to Maximian, before shipping his head off to northern Africa to signify his new status as ruler of all the territories Maxentius had previously held sway over. Although he appropriated all public works undertaken by Maxentius and repealed all his previous edicts and tax increases, a measure which endeared him no end to the common people, Constantine carried out no purges or persecutions of Maxentius's erstwhile supporters.

Having consolidated his position within his own domains, Constantine then set about securing his borders from invasion. Matters outside the Western Roman Empire were still on a knife's edge with Maximin and Licinius at each other's throats, and so to smooth matters over Constantine suggested that he and Licinius meet in Mediolanum and talk peace. Accordingly, the two Emperors met in the city in 313, with Constantine asking that Licinius make good on his previous promise to marry his sister Constantia.

However, the most famous and significant result of the encounter was not the renewal of their alliance but their joint edict, later dubbed the Edict of Milan, on religious freedom. The Edict of Milan was not quite the landmark that Christian scholars declared it to be, given that Galerius had issued a similar edict shortly before his death. In Galerius's edict in 311, Christians who "followed such a caprice and had fallen into such a folly that they would not obey the institutes of antiquity" were excused from their "errors": "Wherefore, for this our indulgence, they ought to pray to their God for our safety, for that of the republic, and for their own, that the commonwealth may continue uninjured on every side, and that they may be able to live securely in their homes."

With that said, the Edict of Milan certainly went further than Galerius did, by declaring all religions exempt from persecution and proclaiming freedom of worship for all, with a special emphasis on Christianity. Not only were Christians freed from any persecution and allowed to worship in peace, but their property (including entire churches) and wealth that had previously been seized in various religious purges over the years were granted to them with full restitution. The Edict stated:

> "When I, Constantine Augustus, as well as I, Licinius Augustus, fortunately met near Mediolanurn (Milan), and were considering everything that pertained to the public welfare and security, we thought, among other things which we saw would be for the good of many, those regulations pertaining to the reverence of the Divinity ought certainly to be made first, so that we might grant to the Christians and others full authority to observe that religion which each preferred; whence any Divinity whatsoever in the seat of the heavens may be propitious and kindly disposed to us and all who are placed under our rule. And thus by this wholesome counsel and most upright provision we thought to arrange that no one whatsoever should be denied the opportunity to give his heart to the observance of the Christian religion, of that religion which he should think best for himself, so that the Supreme

Deity, to whose worship we freely yield our hearts) may show in all things His usual favor and benevolence. Therefore, your Worship should know that it has pleased us to remove all conditions whatsoever, which were in the rescripts formerly given to you officially, concerning the Christians and now any one of these who wishes to observe Christian religion may do so freely and openly, without molestation. We thought it fit to commend these things most fully to your care that you may know that we have given to those Christians free and unrestricted opportunity of religious worship. When you see that this has been granted to them by us, your Worship will know that we have also conceded to other religions the right of open and free observance of their worship for the sake of the peace of our times, that each one may have the free opportunity to worship as he pleases; this regulation is made we that we may not seem to detract from any dignity or any religion.

"Moreover, in the case of the Christians especially we esteemed it best to order that if it happens anyone heretofore has bought from our treasury from anyone whatsoever, those places where they were previously accustomed to assemble, concerning which a certain decree had been made and a letter sent to you officially, the same shall be restored to the Christians without payment or any claim of recompense and without any kind of fraud or deception, Those, moreover, who have obtained the same by gift, are likewise to return them at once to the Christians. Besides, both those who have purchased and those who have secured them by gift, are to appeal to the vicar if they seek any recompense from our bounty, that they may be cared for through our clemency. All this property ought to be delivered at once to the community of the Christians through your intercession, and without delay. And since these Christians are known to have possessed not only those places in which they were accustomed to assemble, but also other property, namely the Churches, belonging to them as a corporation and not as individuals, all these things which we have included under the above law, you will order to be restored, without any hesitation or controversy at all, to these Christians, that is to say to the corporations and their conventicles: providing, of course, that the above arrangements be followed so that those who return the same without payment, as we have said, may hope for an indemnity from our bounty. In all these circumstances you ought to tender your most efficacious intervention to the community of the Christians, that our command may be carried into effect as quickly as possible, whereby, moreover, through our clemency, public order may be secured. Let this be done so that, as we have said above, Divine favor towards us, which, under the most important circumstances we have already experienced, may, for all time, preserve and prosper our successes together with the good of the state. Moreover, in order that the statement of this decree of our good will may come to the notice of all, this rescript, published by your decree, shall be announced everywhere and brought to the knowledge of all, so that the decree of this, our benevolence, cannot be concealed."

Nevertheless, despite this favoritism towards Christianity, there is still no definitive proof that Constantine was a Christian at this stage. Indeed, two years later, when he erected the famous Arch of Constantine, he made sacrifices to Victory and other deities. Though there are religious motifs on the arch itself, as well as religious themes affecting the way it was constructed and located, they are all pagan, and there is no Christian iconography to be found anywhere on the arch.

The arch

In 325 CE, Constantine presided over the first Ecumenical Council, the Council of Nicaea. In his role as *Pontifex Maximus* (supreme pontiff), a role that the Emperors had held since Augustus but now included Christian clerics as well, Constantine presided over the declaration of Arianism as heretical, as well as declaring the Roman Julian Calendar the only valid source for ecclesiastical festivities (as opposed to the more traditional Hebrew calendar). Interestingly, despite this close involvement in Christian affairs, Constantine was still contentedly minting currency representing *Sol Invictus*, with the Labacum being retained as his personal standard, not as an imperial standard.

Thus, it is still technically unclear whether Constantine was avowedly a Christian at this point, but he certainly seemed to have been making an overt show of portraying himself as such. Still, even as he was constructing churches such as the Church of the Holy Sepulchre and the original Basilica of Saint Peter in Rome, he was taking care to ingratiate himself with the pagans by maintaining their shrines, guaranteeing religious freedom, and constructing temples throughout the empire.

Orthodox icon depicting the First Council of Nicaea

It was around 326 that the shadowy figure of Helena, Constantine's mother, reemerged to the fore, this time as the architect of Constantine's policy of religious integration and promotion of Christian rights. In 327, Helena, who was almost certainly a devout Christian with Constantine's blessing, traveled to Jerusalem on a quest to uncover some of Christianity's most sacred relics. With the title of Augusta Imperatrix and the virtually limitless funds of Constantine's royal treasury at her complete disposal, Helena traveled to the Holy Land, where she passed through Bethlehem and established the Church of the Nativity (on the location of Christ's birthplace at Bethlehem) and the Church of the Mount of Olives (on the site of Christ's ascension). According to local tradition, Helena also founded a church and attendant monastery on the site of the Burning Bush before proceeding for Jerusalem.

Icon depicting Constantine and Helena

Once she had reached the holy city, Helena proceeded to the pagan temple that Hadrian had ordered built over the site of Jesus's tomb (near Calvary) and had it torn down, intending to build a church in its place. While the workers were excavating the foundations, they discovered the remnants of three large crosses, which Helena declared to be the True Cross on which Jesus was crucified and the two crosses the two thieves were martyred on. According to legend, the True Cross confirmed its authenticity by curing a terminally ill woman and was promptly taken into safekeeping by Helena herself. Helena is also credited with discovering Jesus's tunic, pieces of rope used to tie Jesus to the cross, nails from the crucifixion, and other relics, many of which would eventually find their way to Rome. Others were left in Jerusalem, and still more eventually were placed in Cyprus. Helena also brought back earth from Golgotha, which was scattered over the site of the Vatican Gardens.

While Constantine's mother was touring the Holy Land in search of religious artifacts and causing his own credit with his Christian subjects to skyrocket in the process, Constantine had not been idle. At this stage, he believed his new, unified empire needed a capital. His old stronghold of Augusta Trierorum was neither grand enough nor sufficiently positioned strategically, and other cities like Sirmium and Rome itself all presented problems.

Constantine decided, in the end, to redevelop the strategically vital city of Byzantium on the Bosphorus. Accordingly, he began an unprecedentedly vast program of reconstruction and expansion which was initially named *Nova Roma Constantiniana* ("the new Rome of Constantine"). In a departure from his previously theologically ambivalent religious policies, Constantine chose to erect only Christian temples in his new city, even replacing some older pagan structures, and placed relics in "religiously strategic" places throughout the city to extend divine protection over the walls of what quickly became known colloquially as Constantinople.

Hagia Eirene, the first church commissioned by Constantine in Constantinople

Constantine revived the clean shaven look, which Augustus himself had favored 300 years earlier. Given his conversion of the empire and relocation to Constantinople, Constantine directly shaped the histories of Europe, the Byzantine Empire, the Roman Empire, and the growth of the Catholic Church. While he was being venerated as a saint by the Eastern Orthodox Christians in the Byzantine Empire, Charlemagne was claiming his mantle in Western Europe about 400 years later, making sure that his own court was adorned with monuments to Constantine. Constantine's popularity even extended to Britain, where 12th century Britons were trying to claim him as a native son by claiming Helena actually originated from Colchester.

At the same time, Constantine was shaped by his times just as much as he shaped them. His decision to regard Rome an unsalvageable capital was the consequence of a deeply rooted pragmatism. After all, Constantine himself had conquered Rome, and in less than 100 years, Rome would be sacked by foreigners.

By 408, Alaric I and the Visigoths were laying siege to the Eternal City, though it was no longer technically the capital of the Western Roman Empire. The Romans had moved their capital to the more easily defended city of Ravenna, but Emperor Honorius still hoped to deal with Alaric's Visigoths in Italy. Meanwhile, the Senate took matters into its own hand by bribing Alaric with 5,000 pounds of gold, 30,000 pounds of silver, and other goods to end the siege. Alaric took the deal and left the region, but before the Senate could convince Honorius to figure out a way to placate the Goths, Alaric was back to lay siege to Rome yet again, in part because Honorius initially tried to use military means to force the Goths out.

Medieval depictions of Alaric's sack of Rome

Somewhat fittingly, the ultimate collapse of Rome benefited the Eastern Roman Empire. Having been cut off from the Western half of the empire, the Byzantines in Constantinople made Theodoric, the leader of the Ostrogoths, the imperial Master of Soldiers and even a patrician in 484, titles accompanied with financial subsidies. Nonetheless, he and his armies still wreaked havoc on the Balkan provinces and all major urban centers there. Since Odoacer ruled the West, Zeno hoped to neutralize the two barbarian obstacles by promising Italy to Theodoric if he removed Odoacer from the throne of the Western Empire. Thus, Theodoric was given the task to restore Byzantine control and rule in the name of the Byzantine Emperor, and he left for Italy with 100,000 followers.

The removal of the Ostrogoths from the Balkans obliterated the military threat they became for the integrity of the Eastern Roman Empire, but in the long run, it caused more problems than solutions for the Byzantine Emperors. Instead of getting an obedient vassal, Zeno was faced with Theodoric founding his own Italian kingdom with a capital in Ravenna after he arrived in Italy late in the summer of 489 and conquered all the lands ruled by Odoacer in three great battles. Ravenna, Casana, and Rimini were the only strongholds that did not fall to Theodoric in 490, so Odoacer resisted for three more years, but a great famine in the besieged cities was the breaking point of Odoacer's power. He was executed a short period after surrendering Ravenna to Theodoric.

Though Theodoric and his people were a politically driving force in Italy, a deep cultural chasm developed between the Goth newcomers and the Roman natives. The groups had different languages, different customs, and different social orders, and the language difference also spilled over into literacy and religion. The majority of the Goths were followers of Arianism, introduced to Christianity by the teaching of Ulfilas (also spelled as Wulfilas), a 4th century bishop who was also Goth by origin. Ulfilas had spread Arian teachings to his followers and translated the Bible into the Goths' language.[1] The oldest surviving copy of Ulfilas' translation of the Bible is the 6th century purple *Codex Argenteus* or the *Silver Book*, which contains almost all of the text of the four Gospels.[2]

All of this would help motivate the Byzantine emperors back in Constantinople to make another play for Rome, but the regional differences already existed, and they would have a lasting impact on the Church. In fact, even as the division of the Roman Empire only formally occurred in 395 by the judgment of Theodosius I (347-395), by then the authority of the Church had already spread across the Mediterranean Sea.

Five Christian Sees arose throughout the empire. These were known as the Pentarchy, and their patriarchs were the Bishops of Rome, Constantinople, Antioch, Alexandria, and Jerusalem. Each was presumed to have been founded by an apostle, but their preeminence over other bishoprics was mostly due to the economic and administrative power these cities had[3]. The Sees of Rome and Antioch were said to have been founded by Saint Peter himself, considered the most important figure in the foundation of the Church after Jesus and also the first Supreme Pontiff. Constantinople's See had Andrew the Apostle, brother of Peter, as its founder.

Theological and Cultural Differences

From virtually the beginning of organized Christianity, ecumenical (meaning universal)

---

[1] Kulikowski, 2007:107-109

[2] The Codex had 366 folios, of which 188 were preserved. Today, it is kept in Carolina Rediviva, of Uppsala University Library. A digitalized version is available at http://app.ub.uu.se/arv/codex/faksimiledition/contents.html

[3] Carson and Catholic University of America, *New Catholic Encyclopedia. 4.*, 299.

councils took place throughout the Roman Empire to organize the multiple local religious variations into a single Christendom, both in its theological and ritual aspects. Relationships between churches were lively in the first seven ecumenical councils celebrated between the 4th and 8th centuries, but Muslim expansion in the 8th century left many Sees in ruins until only the two main centers of Christianity, Rome and Constantinople, remained.

The fact that the main patriarchies were reduced to only two increased the rivalry between these Sees over disputes of authority and about how the Church should be governed. Initially, the two struggled to find common ground with which to establish unity. However, as time passed, each found increasing fault with the other and this led to both becoming more uncompromising and less willing to accept the other as an equal.

The Great Schism itself and the internecine disputes that preceded it principally arose from different theological views that gradually developed between the two Christian Churches. Some of these differences might, to an outsider, seem unimportant, but to those within the two churches they were essential differences in the interpretation of the Word of God. Some were matters of ritual, others were more fundamental. All these major disputes have long histories that predate the schism itself.

One of the main points of difference was the increasingly vehement view of the Roman Church on celibacy. The Roman Church believed that celibacy was essential in its clergy. It was, therefore, completely opposed to the marriage of clerics because if such marriages were consummated, this would violate the requirement for celibacy. The Eastern Orthodox Church took a different view; while celibacy was the norm for bishops and senior church leaders, married men could be ordained as priests. As in many aspects of the differences that gradually emerged between the Churches, both held entrenched and dogmatic views on celibacy which neither were willing to give up.

The other main difference, and perhaps the one that most contributed to the schism that followed, was the *filioque*. Basically, the *filioque* refers to the nature of the Holy Trinity and God. While the Eastern Church maintained that the Holy Spirit came from God alone, the Western Church introduced the notion of the Son (*filioque* in Latin means "and (*que*) the son" (*filio*)) as co-giver of the Holy Spirit. The difference between one conception and the other is subtle and yet of the utmost importance.

Within the Orthodox Church, in addition to denouncing its hermeneutic flaws, this was often referred to as a tautology, that is, that given the nature of God it is redundant to mention the Son, as this is implicit in the Father. Members of the Orthodox Church also believed that this idea diminishes the importance of the Holy Spirit in the Trinity, as well as the theological fundament of the Trinity itself. With the *filioque*, the perfection of the nature of God contemplated in the Trinity, the idea of each of its components having its own specific properties, is unbalanced.

Therefore, the Orthodox Church holds the Father as the sole creator of the Holy Spirit, while the son acts as a medium through whom the Holy Spirit descends. The Roman Church believes that the addition reflects the true nature of the Holy Spirit, having been given to mankind by God but also by the Son, giving emphasis to his participation.

Through the centuries, both churches have defended their position with both citing the Bible as well as the history of Christianity and its councils, making this a philological and historical as well as a theological matter. But, since it touches on something as sensitive as God's very own nature, the Eastern response to its addition by the Roman Church was outrage, and the filioque was only accepted by it in a very few extreme situations. Nonetheless, the theological disputes created by the filioque would prove short lived compared to its political implications.

Though the filioque was perhaps the most important theological difference between the eastern and western branches of the Church, it was not the only one. For example, in terms of the Eucharist, the rite of consuming bread and wine symbolizing the union with Christ, the Churches still maintain up to this day different interpretations. While the Roman Church exclusively uses unleavened bread for the ritual (at least it has done since the 9th century), the Orthodox Church has always used leavened. Choosing one or the other corresponds with the belief as to which was used by Jesus during the Last Supper.

Lastly, the differences between Churches were not only theological or liturgical, but they also had cultural and regional origins. Perhaps the most significant was language. The Roman Catholic Church conducted its liturgy in Latin. The Eastern Orthodox Church conducted its liturgy in Koine Greek, the language in which of the New Testament was originally written. Within the Churches themselves, Latin and Greek were also used for communication and this made discussions between the Churches potentially problematic as in "many of their disputes harm was done by an unintentional error in translation"[4]. Even the most harmless messages could be misunderstood due to the poor understanding each had of the other's language.

Culturally, the two also had significant differences. For the Roman Catholic Church, based in the west where illiteracy was almost universal, the liturgy taught by its clerics was based on a strict, simple, and universal number of practices and beliefs, making admission to the Church and religious life possible even for those who were not fluent in Latin. The center of this approach was the adoption and repetition of a dogmatic set of ritual practices, and this was not questioned as "neither an educated laity nor a public opinion that was articulate on religious matters existed in the West before about the twelfth century"[5]. In the Eastern provinces, a higher general level of literacy and education enabled a more complex interpretation of religious practice and its foundations. The Eastern Church was not proscriptive of this behavior and did not intervene or set limits for it if the situation did not threaten the general social order.

---

[4] Runciman, *The Eastern Schism*, 12.

[5] Ibid., 11.

The fall of the Roman Empire also brought about a regression for the Church, which had become the most influential institution in Western Europe. By the first centuries of the Early Middle Ages, the city of Rome, built to house a population of over one million people, had only around 100,000 inhabitants. Large parts of the former capital had reverted to forest and grazing land. Within this crumbling city, the palaces of the Roman Catholic Church were maintained in the Vatican Borgo close to the Tiber River. In contrast, Constantinople, home of the Eastern Orthodox Church and the center of the Byzantine Empire, remained a vibrant and thriving center of trade.

The Roman Church condemned all activity undertaken for profit, and this led to a further massive decrease in commercial activity in the West. Where before there had been safe routes for caravans of merchants and travelers, now the forest grew back,[6] and this economic and social dynamic would bring about the system of European feudalism. Commercial stagnation meant more difficult communications. With harder conditions for traveling, contact between churches diminished and the rejection of trade by the Roman Church further increased divisions with the Church authorities in Constantinople, who were content to coexist within the thriving trade of Constantinople. In this context, the condemnation of trade by the Romans can also be interpreted as an implicit criticism of those in the East, which was supported by wealthy traders and merchants.

The activities of outside invaders caused even more problems, though these affected the relatively impoverished city of Rome more than Constantinople. A major problem were bands of Slav pirates which operated in the Mediterranean Sea, a communication channel the Church had until then taken for granted. As early as the 6th century, these incursions began to interfere with communication between the leaders of the Church in Constantinople and Rome.

Language and cultural isolation were lessened towards the end of the 7th century when Hellenic Christians moved to the Italian Peninsula to find refuge. In this period, "eleven of the thirteen popes were Greek speakers from Syria, Sicily, or Constantinople"[7]. However, the last of them, Pope Zachary (679-752) would also be the last Supreme Pontiff of Greek origin. It should be noted that the fact that these popes were of Greek origin did not expressly make them supporters of the Eastern Church.

During this time, the Eastern Church adopted iconoclasm, a rejection of icons and other images, from 730-787 and again from 814-842. This was condemned by Pope Gregory II (669-731), and during the Byzantine Empire's two iconoclastic periods, the papacy, which opposed the idea, received with open arms those escaping persecution from the Byzantine Empire. The Western Church "never revered images in the same way," and it was arguably difficult for its concepts to validate the actions in the East[8].

---

[6] Escohotado, *Los enemigos del comercio*, 254.

[7] Noble, Smith, and Baranowski, *Early Medieval Christianities, c. 600--c. 1100*, 217.

Despite the differences, throughout this time, church leaders in Constantinople and Rome managed to maintain a cordial relationship. However, the situation was about to change as the Roman Church became inextricably intertwined with politics in Western Europe.

During the 8th century, Rome found itself under threat from the Lombards, a Germanic people who had taken control of much of northern Italy and were looking to extend their influence over the whole Italian Peninsula. Seeking aid in fighting against the Lombards, the pope first asked for help from Constantinople, but when the request was refused, he met with Pepin the Short (714-768), leader of the Franks, another Germanic people who ruled a kingdom on the Lower and Middle Rhine rivers.

Pepin had made himself leader of the Franks, though by tradition the divine right as ruler over those people was associated with bloodline of the Merovingians, the traditional ruling family of the Franks. To legitimize his rule, Pepin required a decree confirming the legitimacy of his position. The pope, supreme arbitrator of all matters of monarchy, was the only authority that could provide such a decree. This Pope Zachary did, crowning Pepin as the legitimate King of the Franks. The last of the Merovingians and Pepin's only rival, Childeric III, was confined in a monastery. Shortly afterwards, following a request by Pope Stephen II (715-757), Pepin declared war on the Lombards.

One of Pepin's sons, Charles the Great (748-814), added to the Franks' kingdom "extensive new areas including Frisia, Saxony, Lombard Italy, the Avar empire, and a portion of Muslim Spain."[9] Charlemagne spread Christianity while doing so, and on Christmas Day in the year 800, Pope Leo III crowned Charlemagne as the New Emperor of Rome in Saint Peter's Basilica. This is often cited as one of the most consequential moments in all of medieval history, and while the event does spark the collective imagination, what was done on that day was less about a "New Rome" moving forward and more about an acknowledgment of what Charlemagne had already done up to that point.[10]

---

[8] Ibid., 228.

[9] Catholic University of America, *New Catholic Encyclopedia*, 3., 165.

[10] Dorsey Armstrong, *Turning Points in Medieval History, Course Guidebook.* The Great Courses. (Chantilly, VA: Teaching Company, 2012) 25.

***Imperial Coronation of Charlemagne* by Friedrich Kaulbach (1861)**

As might be expected, the rise of Charlemagne was not smooth. Pepin III upon his death had two sons, Charles and Carloman,[11] and they initially split the kingdom, with Charles taking the core of the Frankish kingdom and Carloman taking the lands that had been conquered by Pepin III and Charles Martel. The first issue occurred when an illegitimate son of Pepin named Grifo felt he should be included in the partition of power. The two brothers quickly put down their half-brother, but quickly afterwards they began fighting each other.

Before things escalated too much, Carloman died of natural causes in 771. Carloman did have young children, but, fearing for their safety, Carloman's wife, a Lombard by birth, escaped with her children into Lombardy. This made it relatively simple for Charles to come in and reintegrate this territory into his kingdom. This also created one of a number of possible pretexts for an invasion of Lombardy later in his reign.[12]

Once his own territory was solidified, Charles began to fight wars of conquest and conversion. In total, he fought 54 campaigns over the course of 43 years.[13] For example, he fought a long and bitter campaign against the Germanic Saxons beginning in 772. The Franks had a history of raiding the Saxon lands, but this was a full-scale invasion, with an aim to both conquer land and

---

[11] One scholar notes, with some amusement, that the life of any Carolingian with the given name of Carloman never seemed to end well. Daileader, 26.

[12] Ibid 26-27.

[13] Jackson J. Spielvogel, *Western Civilization: A Brief History to 1715* (Toronto, ON: Wadsworth, 2006), 199.

convert the pagan Saxons to Christianity. This campaign would go on in fits and starts for over 30 years, until 804.

In 773, Charlemagne invaded Lombardy, and by 774 he had conquered the entire kingdom, assuming the title King of the Lombards in addition to King of the Franks.

Even when Charlemagne was unsuccessful, his exploits could become the stuff of legend, as demonstrated by his campaign in the Iberian Peninsula in 778.[14] Charlemagne had shored up his defenses along the Pyrenees Mountains to prevent Muslim incursions and waited for a chance to attack the Muslims, which would come in 778 when the Muslim administration in Iberia was once again thrown into turmoil and chaos by infighting.[15] That year, Abd ar-Rahman I attempted to control the very southern tips of Al-Andalus but was opposed by the main governor of the territory. Although Abd ar-Rahman I managed to expel the governor, he still suffered from numerous rebellions and the resistance of the Abbasids back in Baghdad, who did not support his rule. Thus, when Abd ar-Rahman I attempted to venture further into Spain, the regional lords of territories like Barcelona and Zaragoza decided to ask the Franks for assistance rather than deal with the upstart. In exchange for aid, they offered Charlemagne and the Franks their allegiance.[16]

Charlemagne agreed to their terms and ventured across the Pyrenees with his army, but things did not go as planned. Although the governor of Zaragoza agreed to assist Charlemagne, the city rebelled and refused to let the Franks inside. Charlemagne was unable to take the city and decided to leave, only to be ambushed by the Christian Basques and completely routed. Charlemagne's battle against the Basques would be turned into the famous *Song of Roland*, one of the most famous literary works to come out of the Middle Ages in Europe.

---

[14] Rosenwein, 113.

[15] Collins, *The Arab Conquest of Spain*.

[16] Marios Costambeys, Matthew Innes, and Simon Maclean, *The Carolingian World*, (New York: Cambridge University Press, 2011).

A depiction of Charlemagne's campaign in the *Song of Roland*

However, Charlemagne was not done. As Al-Andalus started to fall apart, he regrouped and targeted major cities like Barcelona. He also claimed the major passes across the Pyrenees Mountains and created several vassal regions, including Catalonia, Aragon, and Pamplona. These regions were directly controlled by the Franks but would eventually be absorbed by Navarre and then Castile to form the future Spain. The defenses established by the Carolingians would remain strong, allowing the Christian forces to eventually cross the Pyrenees Mountains in relative safety.[17]

As Charlemagne continued to rule, he came to understand that, with so many different peoples and cultures within his kingdom, he needed to set up his government less like a homogeneous kingdom and more like an empire that demanded obedience and some standardization, even as it took differences of culture and language into account. He looked at the only great example he knew and began modeling his kingdom after Rome.[18]

One key reason for Charlemagne's success was his genius for organization. It had been said

---

[17] Ibid.
[18] Rosenwein, 113-114.

that when he went into battle, it was not his skills as a general that won victories, but that he successfully organized his forces better than his enemies did. Of course, this genius for organization also served him well when it came to the restructuring of his kingdom.[19]

Through its incredibly successful alignment with Charlemagne, the Catholic Church established itself as an authority over regents in Western Europe, and as two historians noted, "By 1100 the popes themselves often came from north of the Alps, few in the West knew Greek, and imperial authority, when acknowledged in Rome, came from Germany. The Latin world, developing with, assimilated to, and combined with the Germanic world of northwestern Europe, had lost sympathy for imperial and Byzantine ways of ruling while developing its own hierarchies."[20]

In trying to understand what role the Catholic Church played in these early medieval disputes over monarchy, it is important to understand that the Roman Church was seen as being above national politics and the only body capable of delivering unbiased judgements on disputes between rulers. Other than the Church, there was no mechanism whereby nations could resolve disputes other than by war. Because of this, the Roman Church gained enormous influence in western Europe. In the case of the Carolingian dynasty initially represented by Pepin, the Church provided the role of divine arbitrator on who was the rightful ruler. In addition to wielding absolute power over his subjects, the king was a central figure in the cosmological order of his society, considered to have been appointed by God. To confirm this position rulers required an institution dedicated to asserting the right of rule within the divine order. The Roman Church was the only body able to confirm the legitimacy or otherwise of any ruler.

The Roman Church based its right to do this on the *Donation of Constantine*. This document, sent in the 4th century to Pope Sylvester by Emperor Constantine, conferred on Rome's Church the right to crown monarchs, something that had previously been the sole right of Roman Emperors. During his lifetime, Constantine had authorized Christianity as the formal religion of the empire, and though he had not created a single and united Christianity, his authority as supreme patriarch was observed by all churches and he, "for his services to the Church, was raised to the rank of Equal to the Apostles"[21].

In this context, the *Donation* was immensely important in the early growth of the Church because under its provisions, the pope, holding the authority of Constantine, was not only above the other patriarchs of the Church but also above any king. This notion of the temporal power of the papacy would ensure its active participation in matters outside the normal ecclesiastical sphere.

---

[19] Noble, 32.

[20] Noble, Smith, and Baranowski, *Early Medieval Christianities, c. 600--c. 1100*, 213.

[21] Runciman, *The Eastern Schism*, 5.

When the Roman Empire split and Rome collapsed, the Donation suggested that the pope was not under the rule of the Byzantine emperor, unlike the Eastern Church patriarchs. Although they "were nominally elected by their bishops, it was the Emperor, in fact, who appointed them and deposed them, more or less at his will," for "he was the source of law"[22]. Thus, the Orthodox Church, up until the end of the Byzantine Empire, was mostly confined to religious matters, and unlike the Catholic Church, it did not generally extend its influence into the political domain.

A good example of this difference arose from the attempt of the Byzantine Emperor Justinian II to seize Pope Sergius I (650-701) after he refused to sign the terms of planned imperial religious reforms. Historian Roger Collins explained, "When Sergius persisted in refusing to sign, the emperor sent Zacharias, the head of the imperial bodyguard, to arrest him. However, when units of the army of the exarch of Italy and of the Roman duchy discovered what was happening, they mutinied to stop the pope being carried off to Constantinople, and the terrified Zacharias had to hide under the pope's bed and be taken under Sergius' protection, before being ejected from the city.[23]"

Despite its importance, there were some doubts about the legitimacy of the *Donation* itself, and much later, it would prove to be apocryphal, most likely forged in the 8th century. Some would claim it to be "the most infamous forgery in the history of the world,"[24] but during the Middle Ages, it was still believed to be genuine and the *Donation* gave Rome the justification for a supreme authority over both monarchs and the other Sees, including the one in Constantinople. The Roman See thus believed it had authority over all Christians, and that the approval of the Eastern Church was not required to take control of any population.

The *Donation of Constantine* also seemed to prove that papal authority was even above that of the self-proclaimed title of "ecumenical" used by Constantinople's patriarchs since John IV the Faster (d. 595), given that "only the pope had "ecumenical" authority, in the western view"[25]. John's decision to use this term was based on it being used already to refer to Constantinople's patriarchs in the previous century, although never before by the patriarch himself. John held a synod in Constantinople with this title, making Pope Pelagius II (579-590), prohibit "his legate at Constantinople to communicate with John"[26]. Following John the Faster, Constantinople's patriarchs continued to refer themselves as "ecumenical," though they generally refrained from mentioning in communications with Rome, as the Roman Church remained systematically opposed to it.

The dispute over the title held by the leader of the Eastern Church was continued by Pope

---

[22] Ibid., 6.

[23] Collins, *Keepers of the Keys of Heaven*, 118-119.

[24] Fried, *Donation of Constantine and Constitutum Constantini*, 1.

[25] Ibid.

[26] Herbermann, *The Catholic Encyclopedia*, 1066.

Gregory I (540-604), the predecessor of Pelagius II. Having previously worked in Constantinople as an apocrisiary, a superior hierarchy papal representative, Gregory opposed "the name 'universal' for any bishop, including himself"[27]. He was specifically opposed to the "ecumenical" term and rejected its use by the leader of the Eastern Church because he saw this as being in conflict with what he understood as a bishop's rule: to be God's servants' servant. His rejection of an absolute authority for the Church arose from his belief that each bishop was to be responsible for his own jurisdiction. As far as he was concerned, to tread on other bishop's jurisdictions meant going against the central precepts of the Church.

A 12th century depiction of Pope Gregory I

In his various written works, readers can see how he repeatedly preached humility. After him, both popes and kings would consider "servus" (serf in Latin) as an expression of honor[28]. Gregory advised humility not only in politics, but in clerical and intellectual life, "for the wise are to be admonished that they leave off knowing what they know"[29] and also supported managing the assets of the Church for the benefit of the poorest (which, nonetheless, did not stop him from supporting slavery[30]).

The stoicism showed by him differs markedly from the attitudes of later Popes on the matter of Church sovereignty. He proved to be a key figure in the history of papal autonomy. A key example of this is his representation of the Church in dealing with the invading Lombards in 568. Agreeing to pay a yearly sum of gold to prevent an offensive, his role as protector led to the idea of the papacy as the true institution responsible for civil society and its people, and also, to the establishment of the Papal States, which at the time "consisted of lands in Italy, Sicily, Corsica, Sardinia, Gaul, Africa, and Illyricum."[31].

In addition to the divine right to choose a ruler, the Western Church also provided the barbarians with a solid institutional structure, given that "when the Imperial authority broke down in the West, under the stress of barbarian invasions, the only organization that survived was the Church."[32] In this way, the Church maintained effective law and, providing a haven of literacy in a general illiterate Europe, offered to the barbarians its role as an administrator of civil life. The order brought by Christians was to expand to all aspects of everyday life, and in addition to fulfilling a theological need, its implementation was based more than anything on practical as well as civil requirements[33].

Education was also preserved in an almost totally illiterate Western Europe solely by the Church (with the exception of in the Muslim caliphate in the Iberian Peninsula). In a time of general illiteracy, the Roman Church also became, the only institution capable of teaching and arbitrating over clerical matters. At the same time, given its elite intellectual capacity it "continually interfered in the affairs of State"[34]. This was quite different to the situation in the East, where higher levels of literacy meant that theological discussions were not limited to leaders of the Church and the power and influence of the Church was far less outside purely theological matters.

---

[28] Escohotado, *Los enemigos del comercio*, 211.

[29] Gregory I, "The Book of Pastoral Rule, and Selected Epistles of Gregory the Great.", 608.

[30] McCormick, *Origins of the European Economy*, 625.

[31] Catholic University of America, *New Catholic Encyclopedia*, 6., 480.

[32] Runciman, *The Eastern Schism*, 8.

[33] Johnson, *Historia del cristianismo*, 246-247.

[34] Runciman, *The Eastern Schism*, 9.

The influence and power of the Western Church led to the discussion of ecumenical primacy outside of the religious field. As a result, the Roman Church became in the Middle Ages a force above any other secular authority, having ownership and independence and sovereignty that the Eastern Church did not have and probably wanted to ignore when asking for authoritative parity with Rome.

However, regardless of the Western Church's growing power, the Eastern Church had its own arguments for resisting the papal claim to be the sole head of the Church. These can be found not only in the history of Christian faith and its ecumenical councils, but also in the capital of the Byzantine Empire itself. While the Italian domains of the Roman Empire were falling apart in the 4th century, Constantinople became a magnificent city embellished with all kind of relics and objects looted from Greece, Syria, and Egypt[35]. There was also the fact that the economic decline of the West during the Early Middle Ages coincided with the economic growth of Constantinople, and the Eastern Church supported both production and commercialization. In the Byzantine Empire, taxes were sufficient to such an extent that they were not just used to raise military forces, but also to create magnificent public works. Rome may have claimed power and authority, but Constantinople was a much larger and more prosperous city, and that, combined with theological differences, led to a growing reluctance on the part of the Eastern Church to subordinate itself to Rome.

During the same period, while the Western Church had lost its contact with Hellenic culture, the Eastern Church found itself more isolated than ever when large parts of the Balkans fell into the hands of barbarians. The Eastern Church adopted "the belief that their troubles had been God's way of purifying his Chosen People, but if the favor of God and the survival of their empire depended upon their purity, any deviance had to be eliminated"[36]. Thus, the Byzantines embraced isolation as an exaltation of its own values.

After the territorial expansion of the Muslim faith, in which they conquered in little more than a century an area from the north of Spain to Afghanistan and North Africa, Constantinople remained as the last bastion of Christian authority in the Eastern Mediterranean. As a result, its claims of parity with Rome had a strong geopolitical argument. The Islamic boom, as well as the barbarian attacks, led to a "free for all" in terms of the defense of churches, with each finding it necessary to focus on defending themselves rather than aiding others.

The Photian Schism

The Western Church made its way in Europe by going north, and the Eastern Church did the same. Although it had to compete with the Franks in Bulgaria for its influence over the area, Constantinople found in the Slavs willing new servants to its faith. By then, the Franks had

---

[35] Escohotado, *Los enemigos del comercio*, 181.
[36] Noble, Smith, and Baranowski, *Early Medieval Christianities, c. 600--c. 1100*,215.

shown their autonomy with their lobbying to introduce the *filioque* after the Second Council of Nicaea (787). This "Byzantine Commonwealth" succeeded by integrating with local tribes and offering them "a working model, dignified yet also efficient, to would-be monarchs without close cultural affinities or traditions of allegiance towards the empire"[37].

The most notorious precedent for the Schism of 1054 took place 200 years before and began with Photius (820-893) assuming a role as the patriarch of Constantinople in the middle of a period of convulsive political change. He was appointed hastily, as he was to replace a patriarch who had been removed because he was opposed to the new emperor. Therefore, the city was divided between supporters of Ignatius, the former deposed patriarch, and Photius, who sent word to the pope in Rome regarding his assumption of the role of leader of the Eastern Church.

Pope Nicholas I (820-867) stood against Photius's assumption as patriarch, claiming that his appointment had been "settled by a local synod" and without papal approval[38]. Invited by Photius to review his enthronement, Nicholas sent his own legates to observe the situation in Constantinople, without giving them final word on the validity of the Patriarch's assumption, but they ended up confirming Photius as Patriarch in 861. Nicholas I, dissatisfied with the judgment of his own legates, excommunicated Photius in 863, supported the return of the previous patriarch, and communicated his decision to Constantinople. Two years later, the response of the emperor was to invite the pope to stay out of Eastern Church affairs.

This was followed by a dispute between the two sides over gaining the favor of King Boris I of Bulgaria, who was keen to adopt Christianity as the religion of his kingdom. Rather than Rome itself, the Bulgarian leader was approached by Frankish church authorities who had begun to act independently and without reference to the papacy.

The dispute over Christian influence in this new kingdom was an extension of past theological struggles since it included, among other practices, the inclusion of the *filioque* in the Nicene Creed (a document presented at the first ecumenical council in 325), which had been adopted by the Frankish Church.

Later, Photius would be deposed after the murder of the Byzantine Emperor and then again reinstituted as patriarch when Pope Ignatius died. During his second patriarchate, he repaired relations with the papacy. Pope John VIII (d. 882), Rome's new bishop at the time, accepted Photius as the patriarch of Constantinople after an exchange of letters.

The so-called Photian Schism only lasted four years, and its end brought back mutual respect between the two sides, or at least Constantinople's submission to Rome's primacy, as Photius seemed willing to give the due respect that the pope and his authority demanded. During the

---

[37] Angold, *Eastern Christianity*, 6.
[38] Catholic University of America, *New Catholic Encyclopedia*, 11. 311.

following period of peaceful coexistence between the church leaders, the Balkan province of Dalmatia passed into the control of the Roman Church following an edict by the Byzantine emperor. However, King Boris refused to accept this and remained aligned with the Eastern Church. This was a notable point of conflict between the two sides, and many saw it as a direct result of the interference of Photius in an area that rightly belonging to Rome. As a result, despite the peace that followed the schism, "the Photian legend grew in the West, picturing the patriarch as the father of schism and the arch enemy of papal primacy."[39]

The Great Schism

Otto the Great (912-973) was crowned Emperor of the Franks in Rome in 962 by Pope John XII (937-964), one of the youngest popes in history, and Otto was committed to "attempting to recover former papal lands from King Berengarius II"[40], the current king of Italy. This event, considered as the foundation of what would become the Holy Roman Empire, was accompanied by the Privilegium Ottonianum, in which the newly formed kingdom's monarch, in exchange for winning back papal control over a large part of Italy, was given the power to choose the pope. As a result, any elected pope from that time was required to take an oath of loyalty to the Holy Roman Emperor[41].

---

[39] Ibid., 312.
[40] Catholic University of America, *New Catholic Encyclopedia*, 7., 925.
[41] Ullmann, *A Short History of the Papacy in the Middle Ages*, 77.

<h1 style="text-align:center">Otto's seal</h1>

The Holy Roman Empire expanded rapidly and only stopped when it arrived at the borders of Byzantine territory. When Otto was crowned emperor, his dominions included the territories of "Ravenna and the former imperial exarchate, the Pentapolis, Istria and Venetia, southern Tuscany, Naples, the duchy of Benevento and the island of Corsica as well as 'the patrimony of Sicily, if God should give it into our hands"[42]. During the decade after his assumption of the throne, Otto took control of other territory including Benevento and Capua "and had his imperial title recognized by Constantinople"[43] During this period the leaders of the Byzantine Empire were distracted from concerns about Otto's growing power by both a civil war and by a reconquest of part of the Balkans.

The link established between the papacy and the Holy Roman Empire was a matter of growing concern for members of the Eastern Church in Constantinople, who regarded this as "a previously civilized and respectable civilization had been swamped by an influx of barbarians"[44]. The Holy Roman Empire and the Byzantine Empire were the two most powerful confederations in Europe, and to many people it seemed inevitable that they would one day find themselves in direct conflict. With one connected directly to the Roman Church and the other to the Orthodox Church, it seemed that the church leaders might also be drawn into such a conflict.

These concerns grew when several reforms were made by the Pope under Germanic auspices, including the introduction of the filioque. Considered as "the single most vexed theological issue dividing Greek East and Latin West,"[45] throughout the Middle Ages the Roman Church engaged in an attempt to include the term *filioque* in their Creed's depiction of the Holy Spirit, adding it officially in 1014 during the coronation of the Holy Roman Emperor Henry II[46]. The first addition of the filioque was seen in Spain as early as the end of the 6th century, in the Council of Toledo (589). By including this term in the Nicene Creed, the Roman Church recognized that the Holy Spirit comes from both God, the Father, and Jesus, the Son. The Nicene Creed was the result on the one hand of the First Council of Nicaea of 325, the very first attempt to establish a theological unity in the history of Christianity, and on the other hand, it was a product of the later Council of Constantinople in 381. In this review of the Creed, the origin of the Holy Spirit was changed from "from the father" to "from the father and the son."

Charlemagne was the first who attempted to introduce the *filioque* into the Creeds of his churches, and from then on, churches in France and Germany also began to add it. During these centuries, the *filioque* was not introduced by a council decision, but essentially introduced de

---

[42] Collins, *Keepers of the Keys of Heaven*, 182.

[43] Catholic University of America, *New Catholic Encyclopedia*, 10., 712-713.

[44] Noble, Smith, and Baranowski, *Early Medieval Christianities, c. 600--c. 1100*, 215. 222.

[45] McGuckin, *The Encyclopedia of Eastern Orthodox Christianity*, 251.

[46] Noble, Smith, and Baranowski, *Early Medieval Christianities, c. 600--c. 1100*, 215. 222.

facto by different individual clerics. St. Augustine (354-430) was the most famous architect of this conception of the Christian divinity[47].

The ever-increasing influence of the Holy Roman Empire was a critical influence on Rome definitively, including the *filioque*, and this spoiled the relationship between the East and West to such an extent that in 1009, when the new pope, Sergius IV, sent news of his assumption with the *filioque* included to Constantinople, the patriarch responded by not printing his name in the Byzantine Empire's diptychs, the boards which held the names of those bishops endorsed by the Orthodox Church.

At this point in history, Western Europe was slowly entering a period where trade began to return and the numbers of Christian pilgrims began to rise. In addition to Jerusalem and Nazareth, Rome became the main destination for these pilgrims. Moreover, the East Mediterranean Sea became safer as the island of Crete returned to Byzantine hands along with most of the Balkans. This expansionist period led Byzantium to go as far as the north of Syria, and with the safeguarding of these eastern routes, Constantinople also became a popular destination for Western Christians as a stop on their pilgrimage to the Holy Land.

Around the same time, the Muslim leaders in southern Syria and Palestine began to establish trading relationships with the Christian territories. Mainly these were with Italian merchants, who began to establish commercial colonies on North Africa.

All these conditions helped restore communications between Constantinople and Rome. Steven Historian Runciman explained, "Antioch and Jerusalem now maintained a constant connexion with the West, and even Alexandria, which had become the feeblest and most isolated of the Orthodox Patriarchates, could renew her long-lost contacts. In Italy itself Greek monks from Calabria, of whom the most eminent example was Saint Nilus, Abbot of Grottaferrata, and the most unfortunate was John Philagathus, served as a liaison between the Byzantine Church and Rome.[48]"

During this period, changes also arose within Western Christianity, propelled by factions demanding reforms. The origin of these reformist demands can be traced to two movements. The first, the Lorrainers, came from the Lorraine region of France and had the intention of creating a church of marked and administratively efficient hierarchies within a centralized papacy. For them, such reforms required stricter rules for clerical and monastic life, but the Lorrainers lacked a solid base within the Church to push through these changes. The other reformist movement, the Cluniacs, aimed to transform the Church's structure by establishing monasticism as the pillar of clericalism in Christianity, but they also viewed administration and arbitration of the law as an extension of the role of the Church:

---

[47] Catholic University of America, *New Catholic Encyclopedia*, 5., 719.
[48] Runciman, *The Eastern Schism*, 35.

In pushing their reforms, the Cluniac Order followed the orders of the pope, which also meant they were in line with the wishes of the Holy Roman Empire. Certainly, the Germanic rulers were eager to apply these reforms, and it was through the Germanic influence inside the spheres of these reformist groups that the *filioque* was added to the Creed.[49]

For its part, the Eastern Church did not even have the word "reform" within its vocabulary. It certainly went through transformations, yet these were generally intended as a return to earlier traditions rather than the adoption of new ways. This was the case when icons were first removed as objects of worship in Byzantine churches, though they were later restored.

During this time, Eustathius, the patriarch of Constantinople, sent to Rome a document with the intention of healing the growing rift between the two sides. This was part of a movement by Byzantium to extend its reach by establishing churches in southern Italy. The proposal implied the autonomy of Constantinople, leaving Roman supremacy limited to cases of arbitration. Pope John XIX was willing to accept the terms but was stopped by the intervention of the reformist Cluniacs. That movement was already known to clerics in the East, as many of the Western pilgrimages going that way were organized by the Cluniacs themselves.

The relationship between churches at lower levels was actually very good at this time, with Latin churches thriving in Constantinople and other Byzantine cities. However, the differences between the upper levels of the Churches, particularly in terms of the reforms proposed by Rome, were growing, and it was clear that a major split was becoming a real possibility.

Norman mercenaries arrived in Italy in 1017 when a large number were hired by Melus of Bari (d. 1020) to lead a revolt in southern Italy. The Normans helped Melus succeed in seizing the Byzantine catapanate of Italy, and though his campaign did not last long, the Normans installed themselves in the region, becoming not only a prosperous community but also a serious threat to the rest of the inhabitants in the region. This Norman presence in Italy became a significant factor in the later Byzantine collapse in Italy in 1071[50].

The Normans were from Latin Christendom, and the Orthodox churches in the areas they conquered were quickly forced to convert to the Roman Church. The Normans were not acting with the support or sanction of the papacy, and the Roman Church viewed their military successes in Italy with a great deal of trepidation, but their presence caused a deepening of the divisions between the East and West.

In this context, the pope sent three legates to Constantinople to discuss the situation. Both sides had in the Normans a common enemy menacing Italy, but at the same time, the pope's interest did not make him forget that the Normans were from the Latin Christendom. As such, he

---

[49] Noble, Smith, and Baranowski, *Early Medieval Christianities, c. 600--c. 1100*, 326.
[50] Gravett and Nicolle, *The Normans*, 48.

expected that when the domains they had won from the Byzantines were recovered, they would maintain the Latin practices. The mission of the legates, then, was also of liturgical diplomacy, an area in which neither church leader was keen to concede anything to the other.

The leader in Rome at the time was Pope Leo IX (1002-1054), but rather than looking at his position on this matter, it is probably more important to consider the head of the Holy Roman Empire, Henry III (1017-1056). Henry regarded his growing empire and the Church as being of equal importance. The vast size of his empire obligated him to delegate his power to regional dukes. He was keen to do the same for the Catholic Church, but "too often, the bishops he trusted betrayed his confidence and acted from motives as base as those of the turbulent lay nobility."[51]

---

[51] Catholic University of America, *New Catholic Encyclopedia*, 6., 745.

A medieval depiction of Henry III

A medieval depiction of Pope Leo IX

Henry's plan for the Church was to implement the reforms proposed by the Cluniacs. His commitment to the Order was in part due to the fact that his wife's family founded the monastery where the movement began. He heavily influenced the election of three popes selected from the aristocracy of the Papal States, and one of these popes was Leo IX, who represented Henry III's ideal of reform. Leo sent his legates to Constantinople not just to ensure an alliance in the case of war with the Normans, but also to push the reforms desired by the Holy Roman Empire.

As it turned out, the legates Leo chose were not ideally suited to this task. The leader of the legates was Humbert of Silva Candida, who "epitomized the reform movement"[52]. Indeed, he was not only from the north of the Alps but also a reformist who heavily disagreed with the Eastern Church choice of bread for the Eucharist. French-born and a Greek speaker, he was close to Pope Leo IX even before he was elected in 1049, and when Leo IX took the papacy, Humbert was brought by him to Rome and made Archbishop of Silva Candida[53] (today known as the diocese of Santa Rufina). Previously he had been involved in the condemnation of churchman

---

[52] Noble, Smith, and Baranowski, *Early Medieval Christianities, c. 600--c. 1100*, 222.

[53] Carson and Catholic University of America, *New Catholic Encyclopedia. 7.*, 199.

Berengarius of Tours, who articulated the "the first clear-cut heresy in the history of Eucharistic theology"[54]. Most importantly, three years before going to Constantinople, Humbert went on a mission to Benevento in order to win it back for the papacy. It is possible that he had the same aim in mind on his mission to the East.

At that time, the head of the Eastern Church was Michael Cerularius, and even though Cerularius lacked proper theological education, his popularity, as well as his actions for the sake of the Church, made up for it. He was as intransigent in his position as Humbert, and despite the fact Byzantine Emperor Constantine IX was in favor of an alliance with Rome, Cerularius' popularity made him a powerful opponent.

---

[54] Carson and Catholic University of America, *New Catholic Encyclopedia. 2.*, 293.

Constantine IX

A medieval depiction of Michael Cerularius becoming patriarch

The main and most tangible difference between Cerularius and Constantine IX regarded the Byzantine general Argyrus. A Lombard, Argyrus was appointed as Byzantine military chief and backed by the emperor, and he was personally considered a wise choice to forge an alliance with Rome, but Cerularius despised both Argyrus and the proposed Western reforms. He felt that he, as the patriarch of Constantinople, could not lose ground to the Western Church. When Cerularius learned of how the Normans were forcing Latin rites on the Greek churches in Italy, he saw an opportunity to get even by obligating the Latin churches in Constantinople to change their rites. When he faced resistance "he closed them, about the end of the year 1052"[55]. His actions were based on an awareness of the situation in the new empire territories in Armenia, which maintained Latin rites and resisted adoption of Greek rites.

For their part, Argyrus and Leo were already establishing an alliance. They met after Argyrus was released by the Normans who had captured him in Benevento. During this time the pope received a letter from the Byzantine emperor and another from Cerularius. Both pled in favor of a political and a religious alliance. It is believed that the patriarch's friendly tone in this missive was due to the emperor's pressure, but most likely it was actually due to the Orthodox Bishop John of Trani, who spoke to Cerularius in favor of the pope. At the same time, however, the letter contained a deliberate slight to the pope. Cerularius defied the pope by addressing him not

---

[55] Tanner, *The Church in Council*, 41.

as "father," the usual sign of respect for the Supreme Pontiff, but as "brother," and by signing his letter from "Ecumenical patriarch."

If this was not outrageous enough for the pope, less disguised in his contempt was the letter sent by Leo of Ohrid, Cerularius' spokesman in southern Italy. Directed to all Latin bishops, but most of all to the pope, his letter set forth an open dismissal of multiple Latin rites, such as their consumption of strangled meat or fasting on Saturdays. It also inveighed against the use during the Eucharist of azymes (unleavened bread)[56].

To make things worse, this letter reached the pope in the form of a bad translation made by Humbert himself, who, with a mix of poor skills and manipulation, emphasized its already offensive tone. In response, Leo entrusted Humbert with the responsibility to write two letters in response.

On Humbert's way to Constantinople, he met with Argyrus, who advised him to ignore Cerularius and to only deal with the Byzantine emperor. This was a mistake given that the patriarch was immensely popular with the people of Constantinople, but thus, upon their arrival, Humbert and the other legates did not meet with Cerularius. They were limited to being allowed to deliver to him the letter written by Humbert himself in the name of the pope, as well as a letter for the emperor.

The letter, which complained about the aggression against Latin churches and criticized the Orthodox use of the ecumenical title, surprised the patriarch. He had been told by John of Trani that the pope was a reasonable person, and he did not believe that the letter could really have come from Leo IX. Instead, he came to believe that it must have been written under duress from the Normans, probably with the support of Argyrus. None of this was true, but the letter was so confrontational that Cerularius could not believe that it could have originated with Pope Leo IX. As a direct result, Cerularius took the unprecedented action of dismissing the legates, claiming they were not legitimate and did not carry the authority of the papacy.

At that point, news of the death of Leo IX reached Constantinople, and with that, the legates found themselves without authority because Church law specifically forbade legates as representatives of a dead Pope.

Leo IX died in April 1054, and five months later Henry III appointed a new pope, but during this time, despite Cerularius' rejection, the legates from Rome were received by the Byzantine emperor, and with his assistance they translated and published the two letters Humbert had written on behalf of Pope Leo IX. These letters led to a long exchange that, as Constantine knew, would not help the mission in Constantinople, so he interceded and made the local theologians offer their pardon to his guests.

---

[56] Kazhdan et al., *The Oxford Dictionary of Byzantium*, 2., 1215.

However, Humbert did not stop there. Believing that Leo IX would have wanted him to do so, he used the occasion of his visit to Constantinople to raise the issue of the *filioque*. If this was not enough to infuriate the population, on July 16, 1054, during a liturgy in the Hagia Sophia, he and the other legates presented a papal bull "excommunicating Michael Cerularius, Leo of Ohrid, Michael Constantine, the Patriarchal Chancellor, and all their followers"[57]. To make things worse, the bull also made accusations against Eastern practices such as simony and supporting castration, striking at the same time against the Orthodox Church with fake accusations such as alleged attempts at the rebaptism of Latins and allowing priests to marry.

Cerularius took his time in responding, making sure in the meantime that everyone in Constantinople knew of the bull. Public reaction was strong and immediate in response to what was seen as an aggressive attempt by the Roman Church to impose its values and practices on the East. Cerularius' earlier actions, including the closure of some Latin churches, had previously caused some concern, but with the publication of this bull, most Christians in Constantinople came to support his measures.

Several months of negotiation followed without any progress. Finally, Humbert left Constantinople to return to Rome, and "Cerularius responded by convening the standing synod of Constantinople and condemning the Papal legates"[58].

After the emperor had bid farewell to the legates and believed that the alliance was agreed to, Cerularius presented him with a translation of the bull that had been read in the Hagia Sophia. Unsettled by the news of excommunication, and not entirely certain that Cerularius had provided a faithful translation, Constantine had the legates intercepted on their way back to Rome. His messenger asked them for a copy of the original bull, and after verifying that the original text was indeed as inflammatory as the one Cerularius had handed him, he demanded that they return and explain themselves. They refused to do so.

With the wide circulation of the bull's content, riots began in Constantinople, and Constantine found himself the target of censure for the good treatment he had afforded the legates. Seeing how unpopular he had suddenly become, the emperor sought to calm tensions by immediately condemning the legates' actions, punishing those who had collaborated with them during their stay in Constantinople, and apprehending the relatives of Argyrus.

The burning of the papal bull by Constantine's order was followed by a synod to document the whole situation and to do so in a proper way. The Eastern Church did not want to cut all ties with Rome, but it was fully prepared to condemn the actions of the three legates. The Humbert letter, sent under papal auspices, were said to be from the hand of Argyrus.

---

[57] Runciman, *The Eastern Schism*, 47.
[58] Noble, Smith, and Baranowski, *Early Medieval Christianities, c. 600--c. 1100*, 223.

From the synod's perspective, both the papacy and the Western Church were excluded from the blame that was now directed at the actions of the legates. However, Rome's reaction to the synod's message was not as intended. For the most part, this was due to Humbert's powerful influence, which reframed the Byzantine response as a direct attack against the Church. He was successful in this, mainly because of the influence and support granted by the history he had with two individuals who later became popes, Stephen IX and Gregory VII.

A medieval depiction of Pope Gregory VII

Humbert's excommunication of the Eastern Church was then validated, and he continued to hold a high position in Rome until his death. This excommunication marked the final break between the Orthodox and Catholic Churches and the beginning of the Great Schism.

Meanwhile, Cerularius' immediate reaction was to find allies for the Eastern Church among the other three Sees in Antioch, Alexandria, and Jerusalem. He was unsuccessful, not only because there was a strong presence of Western rites in these Sees, but also because the death of Emperor Constantine IX marked the end of his vast influence. Under the rule of Theodora Porphyrogenita (980-1056), political machinations were out of reach for Cerularius, and by the time she left the throne to Michael VI, Cerularius' plans for a rebellion led to him being deposed as patriarch.

The mutual exclusion between the Catholic and Orthodox Churches was not simply theological and political. Most schisms proved to be but measures of temporary disputes which did not last long given that they were based on regular conflicts, but the Great Schism was not tied to such disputes. Neither Cerularius nor Humbert were solely responsible for the schism. They both showed in their actions, nonetheless, a critical part of the schism: the intolerance of each to the other's cultural values. In this sense, "difference" was not perceived as a mere cultural component, but was seen by each as a divergence from their own culture altogether, which they perceived as the only true one.

To most of those at the head of the Eastern and Western Churches, the notion of a divide that would permanently and irreconcilably separate the two was impossible to accept. Most hoped that, as in the cases of previous schisms, the matter could be resolved within a few years, and despite their theological differences, there continued to be monasteries and congregations which had in their liturgical patrimony "texts common to both cultures" since "many of the ideals of monks, East and West, came from a common foundation in Scripture and early monastic classics"[59]. At the same time, not all clerics shared the vision of their differences as a cause for a schism, being "a matter of tradition, not of any divine injunction"[60] and theological differences such as the *filioque* were seen by many as simply different views on essentially the same matter.

On the other hand, just a few years after the Great Schism commenced, a time without Cerularius or German influence over the popes, examples of the deteriorating relationship between the two sides can be seen in the papacy's letters to Byzantine Empress Theodora demanding that she lower taxes on pilgrims. Constantinople also continued to attempt to interfere in Italian politics. For example, in 1062 the Byzantine Emperor Constantine X and the Holy Roman Empress Agnes of Poitou proclaimed Cadalus, then Bishop of Parma, as the antipope of Pope Alexander II.

In 1072, Pope Alexander II sent a mission to Constantinople to discuss reconciliation and the reunion of the Church, but the terms were more uncompromising than ever. The papacy was to remain the head of the social and civil order, and its authority was extended to include the crowning of Byzantine emperors. The Eastern Church maintained its classic model: sovereignty could only be sustained by the five main Sees together, while the Holy Roman Empire's sovereign was to remain as "the Viceroy of God on earth"[61]. Negotiations, although peaceful compared to those that led to the schism itself, were not productive.

One of the first effects of the breakdown of relations between the two sides was the acceptance of the Norman occupation in Southern Italy, land previously owned by the Byzantine Empire, by the papacy. In 1059, Pope Nicholas II took under his wing the Norman Robert Guiscard at the same time entrusting him with the mission of recovering Sicily for Christianity. At that time, the Byzantine Empire was fully occupied by attempting to protect its lands in the Middle East and the Balkans, and "the growing dependence of the Empire on foreign mercenaries, nearly all of

---

[59] Ibid., 224.
[60] Runciman, *The Eastern Schism*, 73.
[61] Ibid., 58.

them Latin, made it highly desirable for the Emperor to be on good terms with the Latin hierarchy, whatever the Patriarch of Constantinople might think"[62]. The reduction of Byzantine domains led directly to a reduction of the empire's economic power and influence, so a war against the Normans was simply out of the question.

In 1073, Byzantine Emperor Michael VII Doukas sent a messenger to Rome. His troops had their hands full fighting in Anatolia and were unable to face the Norman invasion of the Balkans by the Norman leader Guiscard. The emperor asserted that only Pope Gregory VII could stop Guiscard's attempt at conquest. Indeed, he did so, and the peace, though short-lived, was sealed with the marriage of both rulers' offspring.

In 1078, Michael VII was dethroned by Nicephorus III Botaniates, who proclaimed himself emperor and confined Michael's son to prison, canceling his marriage with Guiscard's daughter. The Norman king decided immediately to attack Constantinople, and to do so under the papal auspice, he utilized a Greek monk who was able to pass himself off as Michael VII. Gregory did not hesitate and excommunicated the self-proclaimed emperor, asking for the reinstatement of the true owner of the throne.

With that, a war began. The Norman campaign came at a time the Byzantine Empire was in the middle of a civil war, but Guiscard did not reach Constantinople, giving the reason that the pope required his help in Rome in dealing with Holy Roman Emperor Henry IV. By 1081 the Holy Roman Empire was again secure, though many people were unable to forget the hostile actions of the pope. In response to Gregory's excommunication, Emperor Alexius Comnenus closed all Latin churches in Constantinople, "with the exception of those of the Venetians; for Venice was his ally in the Norman war."[63]

Ironically, despite the fact the Crusades began nominally as an attempt to help the Byzantines deal with the Muslims in the Holy Land, they only deepened existing differences between the East and West.

In an act of good faith, the Byzantine emperor called a synod, and it was decided not only that the Latin churches in Constantinople would be reopened, but also that the popes' names would be written again in the Eastern diptychs. Also, the pope was asked to validate Greek bishops in Italy, which meant recognizing the Eastern Church of Southern Italy as belonging to Rome. The Council of Bari, held in 1098 by Pope Urban II, re-established relations between the Orthodox and Catholic Churches in a climate of peace and cooperation, though the integrated Greek churches kept their liturgical rites and customs. The pope was also invited to Constantinople to hold a discussion regarding the two churches, though this never took place.

---

[62] Ibid., 55.
[63] Ibid., 61.

A medieval depiction of Urban II

By this time, Pope Urban II had become interested in recovering Jerusalem from Muslim conquest and securing the route to that city for pilgrims. Conveniently, adopting a paternalistic defense of the whole Christian world was an opportunity for the pope to once again establish himself as the supreme patriarch of Christianity. With that, he declared that it was imperative to organize "an expedition to go to the rescue of eastern Christendom"[64], a Holy War. A few months earlier that year, he had also held another council in Piacenza, where he allowed two of Byzantine Emperor Alexius I Comnenus' ambassadors to address their need for soldiers for the war they were then fighting in the Middle East.

---

[64] Shepard, *The Cambridge History of the Byzantine Empire c. 500-1492*, 622.

Alexius I Comnenus

Ultimately, the Crusades that began after these two councils exceeded anything that the Byzantines had envisaged. Constantinople became the meeting point for the Crusader armies, and this sparked further friction between the West and East, leading sometimes even to hostilities.

The first of these was the so-called "People's Crusade." After Urban's call to defend Eastern Christianity, and even before the first crusade took place, Peter the Hermit (1050-1115) began to wander around Western Europe exhorting the serf population to take part in a crusade to recover Jerusalem. Peter soon found himself leading a huge caravan of poor Crusaders, yet as they advanced, they gathered more and more people to the cause. To obtain food on their journey to Constantinople they attacked local populations. Although many of them had dispersed by the time they reached Bulgaria, 30,000 arrived at the Byzantine capital.

For much of Europe and in Constantinople, the image of a wandering caravan of mostly poor people without any military background caused fear and tension. That is why, upon their arrival, Alexius I Comnenus lent them ships to cross into Turkey. There, they were quickly massacred by the Seljuks.

These erratic peasants were not the only threat Byzantium faced during the Crusades. The

Crusades, in addition to leading to an important increase of pilgrims to Constantinople, also brought serious hostilities between commoners from the West. Some Western European armies also demonstrated their hostility to the Byzantines by sacking their villages.

The whole idea of a Holy War was even dismissed by some Eastern theologians. Some were concerned that if they did succeed in recapturing Jerusalem, the Crusaders might ask for the pope to come to the city and ignore the existence of the Eastern patriarchates of Antioch and Jerusalem.

Thus, the Crusades highlighted the growing and lasting schism between the East and West. Western rulers found that they could not work with a population essentially of Greek tradition, mainly because of their own lack of understanding and rivalry with Constantinople. The pope was viewed as a traitor to the Byzantine Emperor, who, without being a savior or martyr, had for a long period protected Christianity in the East. For the common people of the Byzantine Empire, seeing these foreign strangers accompanied by Latin Christian priests removed any positive image they might have about the Catholic Church.

Overall, the Crusades provide confirmation of the view that the mutual excommunications of 1054 cannot be viewed as the Great Schism, but rather as a final and decisive manifestation of a long process of cultural and religious separation. Even aligned in pursuit of a common objective, Western and Eastern Christians were not able to find the will for reconciliation. From then on, both sides would remain Christian, but each increasingly came to see the other as completely different, if not heretical.

In retrospect, the Great Schism could be considered inevitable, and linked as far back as the division of the Roman Empire into Eastern and Western halves. By the 11th century, differences regarding theology, language, and culture made a split between the two seem increasingly likely. When two confrontational, ambitious, and entrenched supporters of each side met in Constantinople in 1054, the outcome was hardly in doubt.

Although both sides maintained identical theological destinies in their rites, more than any theological or intellectual discussion, rites themselves essentially were the religion. They were the repetition in which the faithful or common people practiced the religion, and the preservation of these distinct rites could only be achieved by the exclusion of the other. As can be seen in its vast ecumenical councils, all the way back to the First Council of Nicaea, Christianity had sought to overcome its regional differences and obey a single body of religious laws to establish the one and only Church. Thus, each side wanted "ecumenical" primacy.

Naturally, theological disputes between the sides became even less attractive after the Great Schism, as they were prone to mark irreconcilable differences. This was exacerbated by the papacy's meddling in secular issues, something that was never acceptable to Eastern clerics, most of all when a pope declared war or took sides in wars.

In fact, this difference divided the Eastern Church from Rome even when the Turks brought about the end of the Byzantine Empire in the mid-15th century and gave to the Orthodox patriarch rule over all Christians, whether Greek or non-Greek, within the Ottoman Empire. The extent of this rejection can be found in the famous words of Loukas Notaras, the last chief minister of the Byzantine Empire, who asserted, "I would rather see the Muslim turban in the midst of the city than the Latin mitre"[65]. With these words he might well be referring to the fruitless experience of the Council of Florence (1438-1439), destined to be thwarted in its attempts to achieve unity in the Church.

There were times, such as the Second Council of Lyon in 1272, that the Great Schism was (at least legally) repaired, only to be later revoked. In Florence, the Orthodox side was represented by a Byzantine Empire dealing with its decline and hoping to find allies. It was Emperor John VIII Palaeologos' last resort, but he was not the sole representative of the East. Also attending were "procurators of the oriental patriarchates, nominated as delegates by those patriarchates themselves" as well as "delegates from Ethiopia [...] sent by Emperor Zara Yacqob at the pope's request."[66] At the end of the council an agreement was made, but it was mostly at the cost of sacrificing Orthodox theology and its rites. Given its perceived complaisance, this was unacceptable to the Byzantine people, and the conclusion of this council was not promulgated in Constantinople until 1452, when nonetheless it was still unpopular. From these continuing debates and discussions between the two sides, it is clear that the Great Schism, rather than having a precise date, was rooted in old disputes that came to a head in 1054 and gradually became a fixed and immutable reality.

The End of the Schism?
Over 900 years after the Great Schism, Pope John XXIII became the head of the Catholic Church in Rome in 1958. John was a historian rather than a theologian and belonged to the most progressive sector of the Catholic Church.[67] Shortly after assuming his position, he summoned an ecumenical council that would acknowledge the Church's divisions and also try to understand the importance of finding unity again. It was the first such attempt in about 100 years, and the preparations for the council included the following: "Consult the bishops of the world, the offices of the Curia, and the theological and canonical faculties of Catholic universities for their advice and suggestions about a conciliar agenda, to sketch the general lines of the topics to be discussed at the Council, and to suggest various bodies that would prepare the material for conciliar deliberation.[68]"

---

[65] McGuckin, *The Encyclopedia of Eastern Orthodox Christianity*, 256.
[66] Ibid.
[67] Johnson, *Historia del cristianismo*, 670-671.
[68] Catholic University of America, *New Catholic Encyclopedia*, 14., 407.

Pope John XXIII

In this enormous gathering, the most highly attended ecumenical council in history, the pope's main objectives were for Christianity to update itself to adapt to the modern world and address all its concerns globally. To do so, clerics must be able to outline the basis for Christianity above any doctrinal differences and be able to reach not only all Christians, but also non-Christians.

The council, which started in 1962, was attended by representatives of the Orthodox Church who came from countries as diverse as Egypt, Syria, Ethiopia, and Armenia. Although the council did not achieve the "ecumenical" level, as not all churches assisted or had a vote in it, even denominations such as Quakers, Lutherans, and Methodists attended. The remit of John's task implicitly included the notion that repairing the Great Schism was a major part of this desired unity. After all, it was contradictory for Christians to attempt to integrate non-Christians when Christianity could not even find unity within itself. He asked during the council "for non-Catholics to pardon Catholics for their faults in the schisms and condoned injuries done to Catholics"[69]. This was in complete contrast with the previous ecumenical council, the First Vatican Council, which had been held in 1869-1870 and declared "papal infallibility," "the belief that a pope's pronouncements on issues of doctrine and conduct were incapable of being wrong"[70].

The objective Pope John XXIII aimed for was finally attained the day before the closure of the fourth and last period of the council. Unfortunately, he was not there to see it, as he had passed away two years before. Instead, Pope Paul IV, together with Patriarch Athenagoras I of Constantinople, declared the Great Schism to be a thing of the past and announced their rejection of past excommunications. They also declared that they had mutually forgiven and forgotten past offenses.

A year before their announcement, both leaders had met in Jerusalem in what was the first meeting between the heads of Rome and Constantinople since the Council of Florence in 1439. They would meet again after the council in Istanbul in 1967. Since then, meetings between the leaders of both sides have sustained this same interest in a united Christianity, such as the meetings of Demetrios I and Pope John Paul II in 1979 and Bartholomew I's meeting with Pope Benedict XVI and Pope Francis in 2006 and 2014 respectively.

Theologically speaking, the Great Schism was a division that cannot be seen as the result of the heresy of one side or the other.[71] The *filioque's* presence in the nature of the Holy Spirit, as well as the rest of the theological and ritual differences, are mostly respected, or at the very least they are discussed and accepted now. Thus, Orthodox and Catholic practices remain distinct, but with the differences and political interests of the past left behind, Christianity as an institution has found embracing the differences to be the best way to maintain peace.

Online Resources

Other books about Catholic history by Charles River Editors

Other books about medieval history by Charles River Editors

Other books about the Great Schism on Amazon

Bibliography

Angold, Michael, ed. *Eastern Christianity*. The Cambridge History of Christianity, v. 5. Cambridge ; New York: Cambridge University Press, 2006.

---

[69] Ibid., 411.

[70] Collins, *Keepers of the Keys of Heaven*, 414.

[71] Runciman, *The Eastern Schism*, 2.

Catholic University of America, ed. *New Catholic Encyclopedia*. 2nd ed. 15 vols. Detroit : Washington, D.C: Thomson/Gale ; Catholic University of America, 2003.

Casiday, Augustine, and Frederick W. Norris, eds. *Constantine to c. 600*. Vol. 2. The Cambridge History of Christianity. Cambridge ; New York: Cambridge University Press, 2007.

Collins, Roger. *Keepers of the Keys of Heaven: A History of the Papacy*. New York: Basic Books, 2009.

Congar, Yves. *After 900 Years, Background of Schism between Eastern and Western Church 1959*. New York: Fordham University Press, 1959.

Escohotado, Antonio. *Los enemigos del comercio I: una historia moral de la propiedad*. Vol. 1. 3 vols. Barcelona: Espasa, 2014.

Fried, Johannes. *Donation of Constantine and Constitutum Constantini: The Misinterpretation of a Fiction and Its Original Meaning*. Millennium-Studien 3. Berlin: de Gruyter, 2007.

Gravett, Christopher, and David Nicolle. *The Normans: Warrior Knights and Their Castles*. Botley: Osprey, 2006.

Gregory I. "The Book of Pastoral Rule, and Selected Epistles of Gregory the Great." In *Nicene and Post-Nicene Fathers*, edited by Philip Schaff, translated by James Barmby, Vol. 12. 2. Christian Classics Ethereal Library, n.d. https://www.ccel.org.

Herbermann, Charles George, ed. *The Catholic Encyclopedia*. Vol. 8. 15 vols. Christian Classics Ethereal Library, 2005. http://www.ccel.org/.

Johnson, Paul. *Historia del cristianismo*. Translated by Aníbal Leal. Buenos Aires: Vergara, 2004.

McCormick, Michael. *Origins of the European Economy: Communications and Commerce, A.D. 300-900*. Cambridge, UK ; New York: Cambridge University Press, 2001.

McGuckin, John Anthony, ed. *The Encyclopedia of Eastern Orthodox Christianity*. 2 vols. Maldin, MA: Wiley-Blackwell, 2011.

Noble, Thomas F. X., Julia M. H. Smith, and Roberta A. Baranowski, eds. *Early Medieval Christianities, c. 600--c. 1100*. Vol. 3. The Cambridge History of Christianity. Cambridge, UK ; New York: Cambridge University Press, 2008.

Kazhdan, A. P., Alice-Mary Maffry Talbot, Anthony Cutler, Timothy E. Gregory, and Nancy Patterson Ševčenko, eds. *The Oxford Dictionary of Byzantium*. 3 vols. New York: Oxford University Press, 1991.

Runciman, Steven. *The Eastern Schism: A Study of the Papacy and the Eastern Churches during the XIth and XIIth Centuries*. Repr. d. Ausg. Oxford, 1956. Oxford: Clarendon-Pr, 1997.

Shepard, Jonathan, ed. *The Cambridge History of the Byzantine Empire c. 500-1492*. Cambridge, UK ; New York: Cambridge University Press, 2008.

Tanner, Norman P. *The Church in Council: Conciliar Movements, Religious Practice, and the Papacy from Nicaea to Vatican II*. International Library of Historical Studies 72. London ; New York : New York: I.B. Tauris ; Distributed in the United States and Canada exclusively by Palgrave Macmillan, 2011.

Ullmann, Walter. *A Short History of the Papacy in the Middle Ages*. London; New York: Routledge, 2003.

Valla, Lorenzo, and G. W. Bowersock. *On the Donation of Constantine*. The I Tatti Renaissance Library 24. Cambridge, Mass: Harvard University Press, 2007.

Discounted Books by Charles River Editors

We have titles at a discount price of just 99 cents everyday. To see which of our titles are currently 99 cents, click on this link.